table of illustrations

17. Rock of Toullaëron
18. Trévézel Rock
19. Carnac
20. Cairn of Gavrinis
21. Père Trébeurden
22. Sizun
23, 24, 26. Saint-Pol-de-Léon
25, 27. Saint-Brieuc
28. Saint-Egarec
29. Artichokes in flower
30. Saint-Cast
31. Saint-Nic
32. Pontusval
33. Rochefort-en-Terre
34, 35, 38, 39, 40. Flowers of Brittany
34. Morbihan
35. Côtes d'Armor
36. Quénécan, Côte d'Armor
37. Plessis-Josso
38. Beauport Abbey
39. Finistère
40. Forest of Huelgoat
41. Kerascoët
42. Concarneau
43. Dinan
44. Ouessant (Ushant)
45. Aber-Wrac'h
46R. Pont-Aven;
   Chapel at Trémalo,
   Calvary at Nizon
46L., 51. Dinan
47. Locronan

48. Douarnenez
49. Saint-Cado
50. Naval Museum, Brest
52, 174, 175, 181. Saint-Malo
53, 62, 98L. Josselin
54. Saint-Guénolé
54R., 60, 64. Largoët
55. Montmuran
56. La Hunaudaye
57. La Touche-Trébry
58. Trécesson
59. Pontivy
61. Callac
63. Plouha
65. Trécesson
66, 67. Combourg
68. Fougères
69. Trédion
70. Suscinio
71. Caradeuc
72, 121, 184. Fort-la-Latte
81, 84, 85, 91. Menez-Hom Festival
82. Horse Festival, Guingamp
83. Medieval Days, Vannes
86, 87. Pardon of Sainte-Anne-La-Palud
88, 92, 93. Blue Net Festival, Concarneau
89. Golden Gorse Festival, Pont-Aven
90. Pardon of Penhors
94. Trégarvan
95. Menez-Hom Pardon
96L. Saint-Thégonnec
97. Pleyben

98. Josselin
98R., 99. Pointe Saint-Mathieu
100, 101. Cast Church
102L. Tomb of St. Yves
102R. Quimper Cathedral
103. Chapel of Saint-Egarec
104. Rochefort-en-Terre
105. Commana
106L. Church of La Martyre
106R. Notre-Dame de la Joie, Penmarc'h
107. Chapel of Saint-Samson
108L. Notre-Dame, Tronoën
108R. Roscoff
109. Lampaul Guimilau
110. Gargoyle
111. Belle-Île-en-Mer
112. Baie des Trépassés
121, 122. Cape Fréhel
123. Quiberon
124. Trégastel
125. The Needles at Port-Coton
126–136. Belle-Île
127, 162. Pontusval
128. Pointe du Raz
129, 158, 164. Côte de Granit Rose
130. Lorient
131. Concarneau
132. Léichiagat
133. L'Ile Vierge
134. Audierne
135. Aber Wrac'h
137. The *Belem*

138, 139, 141. Penmarc'h Point
140. Belle-Île
142, 143. Concarneau
144. Dahouët
145. Audierne
146, 147. Cancale
148. Arcouest
149. Aber Wrac'h
150. Les Sept-Îles (Seven Islands)
151. Roscoff
152. Concarneau
153. Saint-Guénolé
154, 155, 171. La Torche
156. Morgat
157. Concarneau
159, 163. Plage des Rosaires
160. Plomediern
161. Baie des Trépassés
165. Trébeurden
166. Bréhat
167, 178. Côte de Granit Rose
168. Plounéour-Trez
169. Plage des Rosaires
170. Lézardrieux
172, 173. Perros-Guirec
176. Erquy
177. Ploumanac'h
179. Plougrescant
180. Port-Louis
182, 183. Saint-Servan

table of illustrations

17. Rock of Toullaëron
18. Trévézel Rock
19. Carnac
20. Cairn of Gavrinis
21. Père Trébeurden
22. Sizun
23, 24, 26. Saint-Pol-de-Léon
25, 27. Saint-Brieuc
28. Saint-Egarec
29. Artichokes in flower
30. Saint-Cast
31. Saint-Nic
32. Pontusval
33. Rochefort-en-Terre
34, 35, 38, 39, 40. Flowers of Brittany
34. Morbihan
35. Côtes d'Armor
36. Quénécan, Côte d'Armor
37. Plessis-Josso
38. Beauport Abbey
39. Finistère
40. Forest of Huelgoat
41. Kerascoët
42. Concarneau
43. Dinan
44. Ouessant (Ushant)
45. Aber-Wrac'h
46R. Pont-Aven;
     Chapel at Trémalo,
     Calvary at Nizon
46L., 51. Dinan
47. Locronan

48. Douarnenez
49. Saint-Cado
50. Naval Museum, Brest
52, 174, 175, 181. Saint-Malo
53, 62, 98L. Josselin
54. Saint-Guénolé
54R., 60, 64. Largoët
55. Montmuran
56. La Hunaudaye
57. La Touche-Trébry
58. Trécesson
59. Pontivy
61. Callac
63. Plouha
65. Trécesson
66, 67. Combourg
68. Fougères
69. Trédion
70. Suscinio
71. Caradeuc
72, 121, 184. Fort-la-Latte
81, 84, 85, 91. Menez-Hom Festival
82. Horse Festival, Guingamp
83. Medieval Days, Vannes
86, 87. Pardon of Sainte-Anne-La-Palud
88, 92, 93. Blue Net Festival, Concarneau
89. Golden Gorse Festival, Pont-Aven
90. Pardon of Penhors
94. Trégarvan
95. Menez-Hom Pardon
96L. Saint-Thégonnec
97. Pleyben

98. Josselin
98R., 99. Pointe Saint-Mathieu
100, 101. Cast Church
102L. Tomb of St. Yves
102R. Quimper Cathedral
103. Chapel of Saint-Egarec
104. Rochefort-en-Terre
105. Commana
106L. Church of La Martyre
106R. Notre-Dame de la Joie, Penmarc'h
107. Chapel of Saint-Samson
108L. Notre-Dame, Tronoën
108R. Roscoff
109. Lampaul Guimilau
110. Gargoyle
111. Belle-Île-en-Mer
112. Baie des Trépassés
121, 122. Cape Fréhel
123. Quiberon
124. Trégastel
125. The Needles at Port-Coton
126–136. Belle-Île
127, 162. Pontusval
128. Pointe du Raz
129, 158, 164. Côte de Granit Rose
130. Lorient
131. Concarneau
132. Léichiagat
133. L'Ile Vierge
134. Audierne
135. Aber Wrac'h
137. The *Belem*

138, 139, 141. Penmarc'h Point
140. Belle-Île
142, 143. Concarneau
144. Dahouët
145. Audierne
146, 147. Cancale
148. Arcouest
149. Aber Wrac'h
150. Les Sept-Îles (Seven Islands)
151. Roscoff
152. Concarneau
153. Saint-Guénolé
154, 155, 171. La Torche
156. Morgat
157. Concarneau
159, 163. Plage des Rosaires
160. Plomediern
161. Baie des Trépassés
165. Trébeurden
166. Bréhat
167, 178. Côte de Granit Rose
168. Plounéour-Trez
169. Plage des Rosaires
170. Lézardrieux
172, 173. Perros-Guirec
176. Erquy
177. Ploumanac'h
179. Plougrescant
180. Port-Louis
182, 183. Saint-Servan

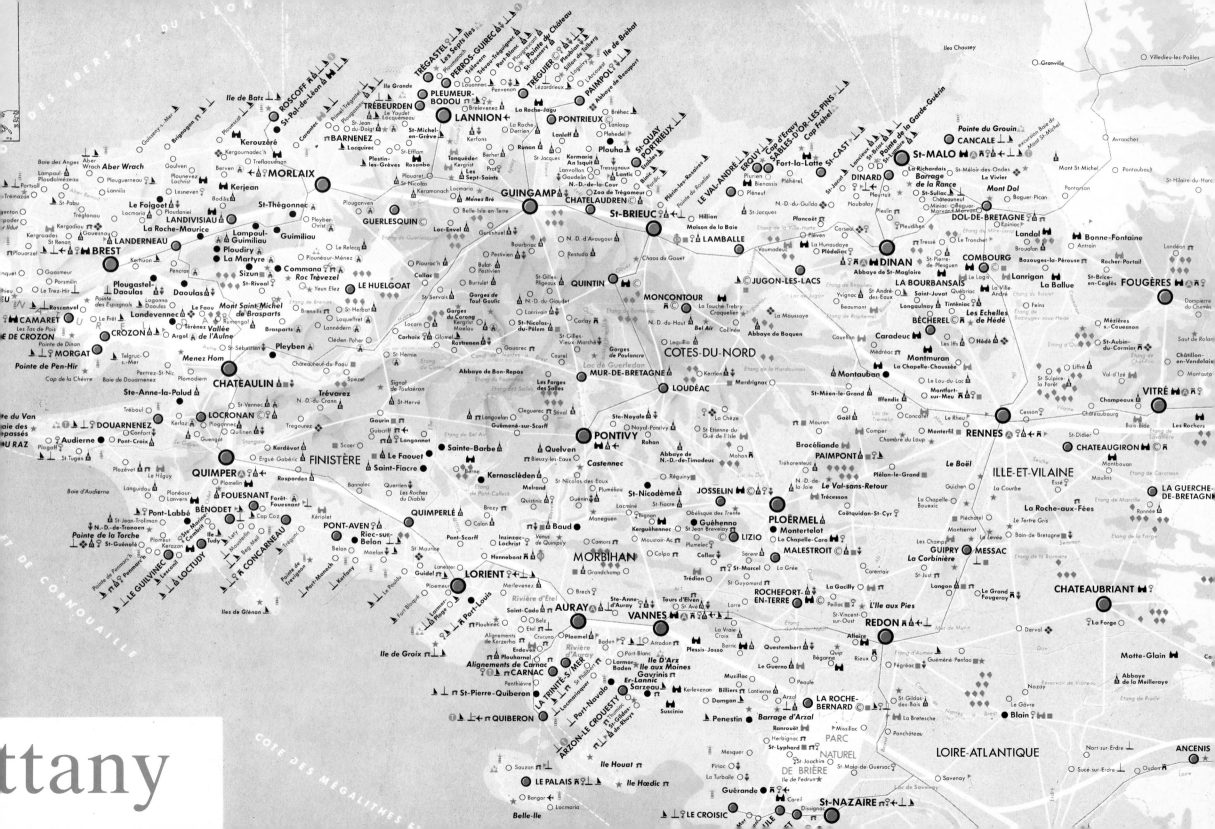

brittany

Photographs by
Jean-Charles Pinheira

———

Text by
Marie Delarue

created by
jean-paul mengès

brittany

The Vendome Press · New York · Paris

For their active aid and steadfast support, the publishers wish to thank:

Le Conseil régional de Bretagne
Le Comité régional du Tourisme

Picture editing: Jean-Paul Mengès, assisted by Marc Dumaine and Frédéric as well as Pauline Debode

Editorial assistance: Arnaud Guillon and Jean-Paul Caracalla

Translation: Maxwell R. D. Vos

Translation editor: Mary Laing

Photolithography: Graphicolor, Milan

Composition: Rainsford Type, Danbury, Ct.

Printing: Grafiche Lema, Maniago, Italy

Layout: Martine Bourigault

Library of Congress Cataloging-in-Publication Data
Pinheira, Jean-Charles.
    [Bretagne. English]
    Brittany/photographs by Jean Charles Pinheira; text by Marie
Delarue.
       p.   cm.
    Translation of: Bretagne.
    ISBN 0–86565–123–X
    1. Brittany (France)—Description and travel— Views. I. Delarue,
Marie. II. Title.
DC611.B848P4513   1990
914.4′10022′2—dc20   90–12671
Printed and bound in Italy   CIP

Contents

Introduction   6

The Land and the Granite   9

Holidays and Holy Days   73

The Sea and the Granite   113

So many painters, writers, and other famous men have acclaimed Brittany that it is no light task to succeed them. There are only so many epithets in the language to express beauty or delight, and used too often they can be rubbed smooth of meaning. There should be more of these words—mutable as the sea, tumultuous as the wind, or bright as the summer sun—keen-edged words for the spiny coast, words to be cupped in the hollow of the hand and poured like gold dust on the sandy beaches. Weighty words, murmuring words, words to take the breath away, words brought from afar to spell out mysteries. There would be rounded words, warm words, words as astringent as the sound of bagpipes or bubbling with bright melody; words unwrapped one by one, pale, stiff, crackling, hemmed with lace and shadowed by flowing tresses. Words to laugh by and words to cry to, words for tempests and words for smooth seas, sailors' words, sailors' wives' words, words from dawn to sunset, words of love and words of sorrow.

Perhaps all these words can be found, and perhaps not; we can but try. We have only to use our eyes: the pictures in this book enunciate many things—strength, feeling, attraction, fear. Above all, passion. These are the ideas which delineate magic, and Brittany is, after all, the homeland of magic.

The immemorial legends in which the land abounds speak no otherwise. Good spells or bad, there is no escape from them; not for the poor sailors taken in Morgan le Fay's nets, nor yet for the souls imprisoned by the alluring Dahut, daughter of King Gradlon, still awaiting the Mass that may one day redeem them, in the drowned church of Ys. From the abyss its bells may yet be heard on wild nights, tolling in time to the endless beating of the waves on phantom ships. And there was poor Tristan, prince of Lyonesse, who went to Ireland to bring back sweet Yseult; never did she set eyes on that king of Cornwall who was to have been her husband, for the love of Tristan overcame her and brought her to her death. More fortunate was Merlin, King Arthur's companion and a sorcerer ensorceled, who lightly yielded up his secrets to Vivien and was by her snared in a ring of magic. For love of her he consented to abide for ever in the forest of Brocéliande; it is whispered that he is still there. . . .

As for us who tread those moors today, magic may fall to our lot as well—snares, love philters, and enchanted stones, for after dark wonders are still abroad in Brittany.

Perhaps these folktales are not as irrational as they seem; perhaps they embody metaphors for those strong passions which, over the centuries, kept France and the duchy of Brittany asunder. Brittany was a much-beloved, much-coveted land, and the wranglings for possession of her fill many pages in the history books; she lies where myth and reality are conjoined here at the end of France, the end of Europe, the end of the world, sprawled cruciform in the sea. Beginning, it may be, as well as end. . . . Here is the birthplace of a mystery never unriddled—the mystery of the great megaliths and the men who raised them; here the last Celts took refuge; hither came invading armies of Romans and Normans; here swords have many times been crossed with our brothers from England. It needed no less than Anne de Bretagne's two marriages and the marriage of her daughter Claude to François d'Angoulême (later François I of France) for the two countries to be united. The coastal province, the Armor, and the inland forests of the Argoat have been the birthplace of many famous people: the gallant Bertrand du Guesclin, the great sailors Jacques Cartier, Duguay-Trouin, and Surcouf, the medieval scholars Peter Abelard and William of Brittany, who chronicled the reign of Philip Augustus. Here was the country retreat of Mme de Sévigné, the 17th century's most illustrious correspondent. Receptive and propitious to the romantic temperament, Brittany produced in the 18th and 19th centuries such men as

Chateaubriand, Lamennais, and Renan, who gave the world one of its most enduring literary schools. She was also mother to the extraordinary fantasist and visionary Jules Verne, to Pierre Loti, to the songster Théodore Botrel, and, nearer our own day, to Henri Queffélec, whose every work echoes the inspiration of his native land. And there were her men of science such as Laënnec and Broussais.

But Brittany transcends her history and folklore; perhaps it is a lingering envy that leads us to portray her so often (and a little mockingly) in such terms. She is also one of the most progressive—in the fullest sense of the word, the most modern—regions of France. Not only has the driving force of technology been harnessed to all the callings of the sea; the inland regions of the Argoat have also transformed their economy in unexpected and impressive ways. Centers of industrial and agricultural research abound. Some of the 20th century's greatest triumphs in veterinary research have been achieved at Ploufragan. Marine biotechnology has its research center and laboratories at Ifremer, telecommunications at Lannion, and so on.

So hospitable is Brittany to innovation that the *télématique*, France's computer-linked telephone data retrieval system, has completely taken over in the region of glassblowers; hogs are shipped by air to Brazil and the U.S.; France's renowned Emmenthaler cheese comes from Brittany's dairy cooperatives. Under the careful eye of geneticists, a new breed of rabbit has been developed, perhaps to take its place one day in Breton mythology alongside the dragon which used to sleep beneath the megaliths and awaken to fly off into the sunrise. It has been said that, like our universe, time is curved into a great circle. There is no yesterday and no tomorrow. History is for ever beginning again; myths fuse with reality, and Brittany sails serenely westward between her two seas, at the prow of the Old World.

The Land and the Granite

Of stones and megaliths

Mystical, arcane, even practical—we may see these monuments in any way we choose, but there can be no certainties. We cannot even evolve a theory without going to the heart of the Breton mystery.

In spite of unending questions, unending discussions in which the irrational is uncomfortably yoked to unbending scientific rigor, our conclusions about the origin and purpose of the megaliths must remain conditional.

These raised stones date back to 4000 B.C.E. and cannot, therefore, be attributed to the Celts, who came on the scene some three millennia later. Certain groupings (in particular the dolmens) were used as tombs, others not; no consistent pattern can be established.

Some have interpreted them as religious monuments—landmarks in some cosmic system. Others see them as survey posts marking out the mysterious telluric currents in the earth's core. There are as many opinions as observers, but no one has yet put forward a satisfactory answer to three essential questions: Who raised the megaliths? Why? And how? The last question is perhaps the hardest, when we remember that some of these great stones weigh 350 tons, or half as much again as the Obelisk of Luxor which was so effortfully dragged to its site on the place de la Concorde in Paris.

_ P. 17 THE ROCK OF TOULLAËRON _

The sandstone and quartzite Black Mountains, along with the Monts d'Arrée, form the spine of the Breton peninsula, and this is their highest point. They are a little lower than the Monts d'Arrée, their crest is narrower, and their slopes are gentler. Once they were thickly and darkly forested, whence the name "Black Mountains."

_ P. 18 TRÉVÉZEL ROCK _

Highest point of the Monts d'Arrée, this rocky escarpment springs from their topmost ridge in an uncommonly picturesque setting. From it immense distances can be seen: to the north the plateau of Léon (Lyonesse), to the east the bay of Lannion, to the west the far end of Brest harbor, and to the south Montagne Saint-Michel, behind which looms the forested silhouette of the Black Mountains.

_ P. 19 _

Carnac boasts almost three thousand of these stones and is the most important of the region's megalithic sites.

_ P. 20 THE CAIRN OF GAVRINIS _

The Cairn of Gavrinis, on the island of the same name at the mouth of the Gulf of Morbihan, is one of the major surviving Breton megaliths. Built during the Neolithic period, it comprises a great rectangular drystone mound surrounding a tomb of the type known as a passage dolmen. The covered gallery leading to the funeral chamber is a little more than 45 feet long, with twenty-three uprights supporting nine slabs. The upright stones are covered with purely decorative carvings, a true masterpiece of megalithic art. The patterns, irresistibly suggestive of fingerprints, are curiously reminiscent of certain Maori tattoos.

_ P. 21 LE PÈRE TRÉBEURDEN _

For several thousand years "Father Trébeurden" has been gazing amiably out on the world under a visor that protects him from the spindrift and the summer sun. He will probably still be there at the Day of Judgment.

And some others:

_ THE MENHIR OF SAINT-UZEC (CÔTES D'ARMOR) _

Its vast bulk is crowned by a crucifix. Carved on the stone is a female figure in prayer surrounded by the instruments of the Passion.

Following a precedent set by Celts and Romans alike, the first Christian missionaries in Brittany tried to stamp out the megalithic cult, but finding themselves no more successful than their predecessors, they decided to turn it to their own account. Pagan ritual was thus able to survive with the sanction of the Catholic religion.

_ THE MENHIR OF CHAMP DOLENT AT DOL-DE-BRETAGNE _

Thrusting almost 30 feet up from the ground and weighing at least 125 tons, this menhir—one of the handsomest in Brittany—is believed to have been brought from a granite outcrop more than 2½ miles away.

It is sinking an inch every hundred years, and the story goes that it will be swallowed up entirely on Judgment Day. The name Champ Dolent, or sorrowful field, harks back to a mythical battle said to have taken place on this very spot, perhaps between Titans with menhirs for cudgels.

And others in Ille-et-Vilaine:

_ *ALIGNMENTS AT KERLESCAN:* ____
540 menhirs in thirteen rows lying behind a cromlech (circle) of 39 menhirs.

_ *ALIGNMENTS AT KERMARION:* ____
928 menhirs in ten rows.

_ *DOLMEN AT MANE CROH:* ____
A dolmen with lateral passages.

_ *DOLMENS AT MANE KERIONED* ____
A group of three dolmens, the first of which has eight uprights carved with stylized symbols: axes, spirals, shields.

The Breton earth

Brittany, though endowed by reputation with a scant and grudging soil, has always been one of the richest farming regions of France. To Saint-Pol-de-Léon, in north Finistère, flows the produce of the fertile marshlands of the "Golden Girdle"—the silty, sheltered coastal belt running from Saint-Malo to the Loire. Here potatoes, cauliflowers, artichokes, young peas, green beans, carrots, cabbage, garlic, and onions can all be grown in the open; part of the crop goes to the major consumption centers (particularly Paris), while the rest ends up in the region's many canneries or is exported to Britain. The market at Cadran handles all the produce of north Finistère; Saint-Pol has become France's most important shipping point for early vegetables. With Fougères, the department of Ille-et-Vilaine has the biggest livestock market in Europe; it is also the country's leading producer of rabbits and exporter of turkeys and guinea fowl. Côtes d'Armor boasts "an endless growing season for battery-raised chickens"; a flock of more than 16 million roosters and hens makes this department the main poultry breeder in France, and indeed in Europe. It is worth reflecting on the advanced technology of the plants, which every year ship almost one-and-a-half billion eggs to our kitchens, untouched by human hand from the moment of conception to the housewife's shopping cart.

_ *P. 22 SAINTE-ANNE* ____
St. Anne's Chapel outside Sizun, in Finistère.

_ *PP. 23, 24, 26* ____
Growing artichokes at Saint-Pol-de-Léon.

_ *PP. 25, 27* ____
Fields near Saint-Brieuc.

_ *P. 28* ____
Country shrine at Saint-Egarec.

_ *P. 29* ____
Artichokes in flower at Kerjean (Finistère).

_ *P. 30* ____
Wheat fields near Saint-Cast.

_ *P. 31* ____
Saint-Nic.

_ *P. 32* ____
Fields near the point and lighthouse at Pontusval (Côtes d'Armor).

_ *P. 33* ____
Tilling the fields near Rochefort-en-Terre (Morbihan)

_ *PP. 34, 35, 38, 39, 41*
THE FLOWERS OF BRITTANY ____
Tidy and clean it stands. Gray or white— gray of raw granite, white of limewash. If the shutters are blue, perhaps it's in Ushant; if yellow or green, in Quimper. Where the houses huddle together against the wind, the sea's nearby; where they make merry on the greensward

Brocéliande, Paimpont, and Merlin
are not far away.
Here's a house knee-high in hydrangeas,
which must be the priest's; this window
smiling through lips of boxed geranium,
flirting under its bonnet of slate—at whom
is it making eyes? At what sailor man
returned from a voyage–around the Horn?
to Newfoundland? shrimping?

For a rejected suitor,
here's a bouquet of thistles,
and for all my much-loved Bretons, two
nosegays of artichokes.

_ *P. 34 (R. & L.)*
Morbihan in flower.

_ *P. 35*
Flower garden in Côtes d'Armor.

_ *P. 36*
Forest in Quénécan (Côtes d'Armor).
Afternoon of a faun.

_ *P. 38*
Hydrangeas at Beauport Abbey
(Côtes d'Armor).

_ *P. 39*
Flowers at a dormer window and a stone
roof, Finistère.

_ *P. 40 THE FOREST OF HUELGOAT*
Now incorporated in the regional nature
reserve of Armorique (the Roman name for
Brittany was Armorica), this forest, with its
lakes, flowing streams, and tumbled rocks, is
one of the most beautiful parts of inland
Brittany; it appeals to fishermen and
backpackers alike.

_ *P. 41*
Thatched cottage at Kerascoët.

_ *P. 42 Slate roof at Concarneau*

_ *P. 43 Dinan (Côtes d'Armor)*

_ *P. 44 MILL AT KARAES,*
ÎLE D'OUESSANT (USHANT)
Firmly planted on its rocky base on the
moor, this mill once ground to every wind
that blows. The sea wind driving a fine rain
before it from the southwest, the terrible
kornog from the west, the gusty *gwarlarn*
northwester—all these have filled its sails,
turned its millstone, and ground the barley
flour from which Ushanters baked their
bread as recently as the turn of the century.

_ *P. 45*
Crêperie (pancake house) in Aber-Wrac'h.

_ *P. 46 R. PONT-AVEN*
The "wild man" Gauguin dreamed of nature
unspoiled. He was told of a little place in
Finistère with a budget-priced inn run by a
young Breton woman called Marie-Jeanne
Gloanec, where many painters from France
and abroad were paying 65 francs a month
for board and lodging. So in June 1886 Paul
Gauguin set out for Pont-Aven. He returned
there often until 1894, to find (in his own
words) "the wild and primitive."
   The young artists clustering around him,
such as Charles Laval, Emile Bernard,
Charles Filiger, Meyer de Haan, and
Armand Seguin, later came to be known
collectively as the School of Pont-Aven.
   It was in a grove at Pont-Aven that in
1888 Gauguin gave Paul Sérusier a lesson in

painting which eventually gave birth to the
Nabis—the artists who, drawing their
inspiration from both Gauguin's Synthetism
and the Symbolist aesthetic, revolutionized
the decorative techniques of stained glass,
lithography, etc.

_ *THE CHAPEL AT TRÉMALO*
This Breton country church, dating from the
early 16th century, is delightfully embowered
in greenery. Inside there is a 17th-century
Christ in wood, which Gauguin took as the
model for his "Yellow Christ," whose
background depicts the village of Pont-Aven.

_ *THE NIZON CALVARY*
This little church, 2 miles outside Pont-
Aven, has a Romanesque calvary, which
Gauguin used in his "Green Christ."

_ *P. 46 L., 51 THE OLD TOWN, DINAN*
It was here that the gallant knight Bertrand
du Guesclin captured the heart of beautiful
Tiphaine Raguenel after her brother,
Olivier, had worsted the dreaded Canterbury
in single combat. This was at the siege of
Dinan in 1359, and the scoundrelly
Englishman was drummed out of his own
army, proving that among gentlemen virtue
always triumphs.... As well as the château
of the duchesse Anne, built by the dukes of
Brittany in the 14th and 15th centuries,
Dinan has been able to preserve its medieval
fortified city, all bedecked with trees and
gardens, at the cliff edge of a plateau rising
almost 250 feet above the River Rance.

_ *P. 47 HANDICRAFTS AT LOCRONAN*
Locronan is a craftsmen's town. Once upon
a time its livelihood was sail making, and in

the 17th century it reached heights of prosperity. Now there is no whaling fleet of schooners and cutters with their home ports in Brittany—but the craftsmen are still there. In today's Locronan linen, silk, wool, and cotton are handwoven, glass is blown, and above all wood is carved.

P. 48 DOUARNENEZ

"Douar an enez," the land of the island, was known as the hamlet of Saint-Michel and then, at the beginning of the 16th century, the town of Île Tristan. The town of today, comprising the communes of Douarnenez, Ploaré, Pouldavid, and Tréboul, has become one of the busiest fishing ports on the Breton coast (mackerel, sardines, tuna, shellfish) and the most important center of lobster fishing in France. There is also a big canning industry; Brittany accounts for two-thirds of total French production.

P. 49 COTTAGE ON THE ÉTEL AT SAINT-CADO

The old Templars' chapel is one of the rare Romanesque structures in Morbihan. The hard of hearing used to come here from all around, asking St. Cado to intercede for a cure. "Cado" sounds very like cadeau, the French for "gift"; a saint with so beneficent a name no doubt heard and answered the prayers of the faithful.

P. 50 BREST

One of the great naval bases of France, Brest owes its importance to its extraordinary situation in the valley of the Penfeld. The long, winding, sheltered estuary was eminently suited to the building of wooden ships, but the constantly growing scale of naval construction required cutting through bedrock, leveling hills, and finally, in the 19th century, building a mole parallel to Laninon Beach enclosing a huge, sheltered roadstead. In 1970 two spurs were added to the main jetty for the docking of aircraft carriers, cruisers, and missile-launching frigates. The roadstead, now covering almost 40 square miles and from 30 to 60 feet deep, is connected to the sea by a steep-sided channel three miles long and more than a mile wide. The topography explains why Brest has enjoyed such consequence as a naval port for more than two millennia.

The Recouvrance Bridge is the largest lift-bridge in Europe; the 280-foot steel span moves up and down between four 220-foot towers above the quays of the naval dockyard. The light units of the Atlantic Fleet are based here. In the background is the submarine base, no longer in service.

THE NAVAL MUSEUM

Housed in the towers of the castle, the museum displays valuable ship models, navigational instruments, and pictures of the glorious days of sail in the 18th century.

PP. 52, 174, 175, 181 SAINT-MALO

As the saying goes, "I'm not French, I'm not Breton—I'm from Saint-Malo," and it may be because the people of Saint-Malo think themselves special that they have in fact become so!

Few towns can boast so many famous offspring. From Jacques Cartier to Chateaubriand (who is buried in the splendid isolation of Grand-Bé), there is a long list of men of letters, doctors, and famous pirates who carried their names, and the name of their native town, to the ends of the earth.

The fine natural harbor and the marked rise and fall of the tides, particularly along the Rance estuary, made Saint-Malo an important commercial port at a very early date. Home of the Newfoundland fishing fleet, this is now the last place in Brittany that still sends boats out after cod—the only deep-sea fishing in the true sense of the word. Its fleets work the Newfoundland, Labrador, and Greenland Banks. Saint-Malo is the third largest port for salted codfish, and the largest for frozen codfish, in the country.

The town lies inside a defensive quadrangle with a round tower at each corner; along the northeast face runs a triangular work known as the Galley, built between the 14th and 19th centuries. The 130-foot-high "great keep," built in 1424 by Jean V, duke of Brittany, is the oldest part of the castle. The four corner towers are later; "The General's Wife," "La Quinquengrogne," the "Ladies' Tower," and the "Mill Tower" date from the end of the 15th century. The castle was completed by Vauban.

The ramparts overlooking the harbor from the south, east, and north were rebuilt in the 18th century, also to Vauban's design; those between the Bidouane Tower and Fort-à-la-Reine on the northwest were restored in the 19th century. Only the curtain walls on the west, or ocean, side, known as the "little walls," between the Holland Battery and the Bidouane Tower are older. The section between Notre-Dame and the Magazine is 14th-century. All these walls have been restored after sustaining heavy damage during World War II.

Châteaux

The castles of Brittany rarely speak to us of peaceful country life; they are built of the granite native to the region, and that kind of gray casts its own chilly shadow.

Breton castles have little to do with the Renaissance or the banks of the Loire or the white glint of limestone.

They are, rather, sturdy relics of the Middle Ages—strongholds, towns girt with stout ramparts, frowning fortresses raised along the coast against the English invader or along the inland marches against the kings of France. They tell no tale of pleasure or comfort; rather of endless sieges and hand-to-hand combat amid the clash of lances and armor.

Even within, few enough are half-fortress half-palace like Josselin; the nobles of Brittany were not rich. Her country gentlemen lived in the kind of modest manor house, a "yeoman's manor," still to be found all across Léon. They tilled their fields; their gentility lay only in wearing a sword.

_ P. 37 CHÂTEAU DU PLESSIS-JOSSO
Or how the fortified dwelling evolved into the Louis XIII country house, as comfort superseded security.

_ PP. 53, 62, 98 L. CHÂTEAU DE JOSSELIN
Built in 1105 by Guthenoc, vicomte de Perhoët, and destroyed by King Henry II of England in 1168, the castle was rebuilt by the vicomte Eudon. It was occupied in 1370 by the Captains Beaumanoir and Clisson, before passing into the hands of the Rohan family where it has remained since the 15th century.

With its steep sides rising straight from the waters of the Oust, its lofty towers, its machicolations, and its curtain walls, which make it look as a stronghold should, Josselin is one of the great achievements of feudal architecture during the Renaissance.

_ PP. 54 R., 60, 64 FORTERESSE DE LARGOËT
Of Largoët castle, which belonged to Marshal de Rieux, adviser to the duc François II and then guardian of the duke's daughter Anne de Bretagne, there remain only the two Elven towers. When Charles VIII invaded Brittany in 1488, all de Rieux's strongpoints, including this one, were burned or razed. The keep, an irregular octagon rising 185 feet from the floor of the moat, has walls 20 to 33 feet thick at the base; it is one of the highest keeps in France.

_ P. 55 CHÂTEAU MONTMURAN
Founded in 1036 and rebuilt from the 12th to the 14th centuries, Montmuran is where du Guesclin was dubbed knight in 1354 after a brisk encounter with the English. He returned there later to marry his second wife, Jeanne de Laval.

_ P. 56 CHÂTEAU DE LA HUNAUDAYE
Built in 1220 by Olivier de Tournemine, the fortress was severely damaged during the War Between the Two Jeannes. Rebuilt and enlarged by the lords of Tournemine and improved during the 17th century by Sébastien de Rosmadec, it was pulled down and then burned during the Revolution. Its tumbled stones were still being stolen as late as 1930, when it became the property of the French state.

_ P. 57 CHÂTEAU DE LA TOUCHE-TRÉBRY
In Côtes d'Armor.

_ P. 58 CHÂTEAU DE TRÉCESSON
Probably built towards the end of the 14th century by Jean de Trécesson, chamberlain to the duc Jean IV, the castle is unusual not only for its medieval architecture but also for the reddish schist used in its construction.

_ P. 59 CHÂTEAU OF THE ROHANS AT PONTIVY
It is not known when the château was built—we may suppose at the same time as the town, in the 12th century. In 1342 it was captured and razed by Montfort because the vicomte de Rohan was a supporter of Charles de Blois. In 1485 the vicomte Jean II built the present fortress which, despite numerous ravages, retains its commanding air and is a fine example of the military architecture of the period.

_ P. 61
Château de Callac, Morbihan.

_ P. 65
Château de Trécesson, Morbihan.

_ PP. 66, 67 CHÂTEAU DE COMBOURG
"We came upon a valley in whose depths could be seen, near a pond, the spire of a village church; the towers of a feudal castle thrust up through a wood bathed in the light

of the setting sun. . . . From its courtyard at the foot of a slight declivity the castle towered between two clumps of trees. Its strong, stern facade was a curtain wall surmounted by a covered gallery, battlemented and machicolated, which linked two towers of differing date, height, size, and construction. Each of these rose to a crenellation with a pointed roof above it, like a hennin encircled by a Gothic crown. . . . Above the gateway were the arms of the lords of Combourg, and the apertures through which once passed the supports and chains of the drawbridge. . . . Add that the structure was riddled throughout with secret passages and stairways, cells and donjons, a labyrinth of covered and uncovered passageways, and walled tunnels whose branchings were known to no man living; everywhere silence, darkness, and a countenance of stone. Such was the château de Combourg." Or so, at least, it appeared to the young Chateaubriand (see *Mémoires d'outre-tombe*) when he first came here on vacation, probably around 1780. Built in the 11th century and restored in the 14th and 15th centuries, the château de Combourg belonged to the du Guesclin family until the 18th century, when it became the property of the comte de Chateaubriand, father of François-René. It has been suggested, probably with truth, that this isolated place, along with the menacing setting which the count provided for his family, helped to develop qualities of sensibility and imagination in the young writer who was to make Combourg famous as the birthplace of French romanticism.

The centuries-old trees in the park recently fell victim to one of Brittany's terrible southwesterly gales.

P. 68 CHÂTEAU DE FOUGÈRES

The Gobelin and Mélusine towers, château de Fougères. A frontier town and military strongpoint of importance during the Middle Ages, Fougères was the key to the defense of the duchy. Construction of the castle was begun at the end of the 12th century and finished in the 13th when the fief passed to the lords of Lusignan in Poitou. They heightened the curtain wall and crowned it with a new machicolated parapet walk; at the same time they built the Mélusine tower, named after the beautiful fairy from whom the family claimed to be descended.

P. 69

Château de Trédion, Morbihan.

P. 70

Château de Suscinio, near Sarzeau on the Gulf of Morbihan.

P. 71 CHÂTEAU DE CARADEUC

In the 18th century this was the seat of the famous procurator-general Louis René, marquis de Caradeuc de la Chalotais, known as the staunch opponent of Governor d'Aiguillon, who persuaded the Parlement of Rennes to vote the dissolution of the Jesuits, then very powerful in Brittany. This struck a blow at the very base of Louis XV's authority and is generally perceived as a prelude to the Revolution.

The château's northern terrace overlooks Dinan and the valley of the Rance.

PP. 72, 121, 184 FORT-LA-LATTE

"Seigneur secourable, château redoutable" (a helping hand and a strong castle) was the motto of the Goyon family, lords of Matignon, who built the castle in the mid-14th century. It looks properly feudal, and the site is picturesque because the building is cut off from the mainland by two crevasses, to be crossed only on drawbridges. The keep, built after 1341 during the War of the Breton Succession, looks out over the sea from its height of almost 200 feet, with an extraordinary view of Cape Fréhel and the bay. Since the castle controls the roadstead of La Fresnaye, it is the key to Saint-Malo.

P. 104

Château de Rochefort-en-Terre. Granite Madonna.

And in Ille-et-Vilaine

LES ROCHERS-SÉVIGNÉ

"Would you like to know where I was today? I was at the place Madame, and went twice around the mall with the players. . . . I could wish you had so pretty a promenade at Grignan. Soon I shall walk to the end of the great avenue to see Pilois, who is making us a fine, gentle, grassy bank sloping down to the gate that leads to the highroad."
Les Rochers, June 1685

In the letters she wrote to her daughter almost every day, the marquise de Sévigné tells us of her life at Les Rochers, where she lived almost continually from 1678 until she rejoined her daughter at Grignan. The château, built in the 15th century and repeatedly altered until the 19th, still retains its magnificent gardens by Lenôtre.

18-19

22-23

42-43

44-45

48-49

62-63

Holidays and Holy Days

Pardons and fetes

The former are not necessarily altogether Christian nor the latter wholly pagan, which means that they must be considered together. And then a fete often follows a pardon, no doubt because it seems appropriate to sweeten with some fleshly pleasure the mortifications inflicted on the spirit.

Breton pardons are, like so many things here, peculiar to this part of the world, differing in many respects from pilgrimages that take place elsewhere, to other shrines.

The most striking thing about Breton pardons is how many there are, and how deep is the religious fervor to which they bear witness. They take place in churches or chapels consecrated to them by a tradition that sometimes goes back ten centuries. The faithful who perform them are promised remission of their sins, the offering of an intention, or some special grace.

The greater pardons are impressive indeed, involving processions across the moors with candles, banners, statues, and relics borne by men or by young women in folk dress. Then come the clergy in full canonicals and a throng of pilgrims singing hymns.

Feast days, too, are on a larger scale here than elsewhere: feast days for the sea, for the boats, flower festivals, medieval days. They embody the living vigor of regional tradition, so cherished by all good Bretons.

COIFS

They are to be seen all over: in Cornouaille, in Léon (which is Lyonesse), in the Trégorrois and around Vannes, near the forest of Brocéliande, and even on the isle of Ushant. Children, their mothers, and their grandmothers all wear the coif—for its good looks, for its regional identity, for its very explicit symbolism—there are so many assertions the coif can make! There are sixty-six principal kinds of costume and coif, corresponding to the ancient "clans" or greatly extended families that once served to define a person's social context. To these, however, must be added the *giz*, or local variants, whence the saying "kant bro kant giz—kant parrez kant illiz," or "a hundred countries, a hundred headdresses; a hundred parishes, a hundred churches." The coif denoted the wearer's economic and social class, and her status as maid, wife, or widow. The varieties of coif are beyond numbering—and certainly beyond distinguishing!

One of the most becoming coifs is worn in Pont-Aven and La Trinité-sur-Mer; the colored headband, attractively trimmed with lace, is set off by a large starched collar. The oddest, and perhaps the best known, is the towering lace coif of Pont-l'Abbé in Finistère, a full 16 inches high; once it used to be of more reasonable proportions, but since 1930 it has grown inordinately. The Quimper coif is smaller and worn on the crown of the head. At Plougastel the coif looks like a medieval hennin, and is tied under the chin with a flurry of ribbons. At one place it is clipped to a chignon, at another worn on the forehead.

But no discussion of coifs and regional costume, or indeed of feast days, can be complete without a mention of the *biniou*, the Breton bagpipe, rooted as it is in the Breton way of life. Influenced by the Scottish bagpipe, although it is played a little differently, the bagpipe survives in Celtic Brittany in two forms. The little biniou, also known as the "old biniou," or *biniou koz*, has only one drone and is used to accompany a separate chanter; the musicians walk two by two, one playing the melody on a chanter and the other blowing into the leather bag of the *biniou koz* and nudging it with his elbow to expel air through the drone. The other, the "big biniou," or *biniou braz*, has three drones, and is played by groups like Scottish pipe bands.

_ PP. 81, 84, 85, 91
MENEZ-HOM FESTIVAL _____

On this outlying peak of the Black Mountains takes place every August 15 the folk festival of the Menez-Hom. It is a kind of marriage of earth and air; there is dancing on the moor, and the bagpipes are played upward towards the sky.

_ P. 82 GUINGAMP:
THE HORSE FESTIVAL _____

Of the medieval city and its ramparts, which were pulled down by order of Richelieu, there remain only some stones and a ruined château. Today Guingamp is a fast-growing industrial town. It has two famous festivals: the horse festival, and the festival of St. Loup with Breton dancing.

_ P. 83 MEDIEVAL DAYS
AT VANNES _____

In the same vein as Dinan's Rampart Festival, Vannes offers its Medieval Days, reenacting the court of Anne de Bretagne with jousting, troubadours, tourneys on the ramparts, and demonstrations of medieval crafts.

_ PP. 86, 87 PARDON OF
SAINTE-ANNE-LA-PALUD _____

"Dead or alive, every Breton must go at least once to Sainte-Anne." Devotion to the mother of the Virgin was brought back to the West by returning crusaders; in Brittany, where it enjoyed the protection of the duchesse Anne and benefited from her memory, it rose to unusual heights of religious fervor.

St. Anne is held to be the patron saint of Brittany. They say that she was a princess from Cornouaille who was snatched up by angels and carried to Nazareth so that she could escape from her brutal husband. After giving birth to the Virgin, she came back to Brittany to die. It was Christ himself who, visiting his grandmother, caused the holy spring of Sainte-Anne-la-Palud to flow.

_ PP. 88, 92, 93 FESTIVAL OF
THE BLUE NETS, CONCARNEAU _____

First held in 1905 in aid of sardine fishermen and their families, this celebration has, over time, become one of folklore rather than philanthropy.

_ P. 89 GOLDEN GORSE FESTIVAL,
PONT-AVEN _____

This gorse-flower festival was begun by Théodore Botrel at the turn of the century.

_ P. 90 _____

Penhors Pardon, on the shore of Audierne Bay (Finistère)

_ P. 95 THE MENEZ-HOM PARDON
in the Black Mountains of Finistère _____

Held at Notre-Dame-du-Haut, the chapel of the seven healer saints. There are wooden statues of St. Mamert, invoked against colic; Sts. Yvertin and Eugénie (or Tujanne), sovereign against migraine; St. Lubin for diseases of the eye; St. Méen for madness; St. Hubert for wounds and dog bites; St. Houarniaule for fear.

With so many openhanded patrons, it is not surprising that the Menez-Hom pardon is one of the most popular.

And some others...

_ THE LESSER TROMÉNIE,
LOCRONAN _____

Locronan is famous for its pardons, known locally as Troménies. The greater Troménie is held every six years. Banner-carrying pilgrims make a 7½-mile circuit of the mountain, reenacting the walk which St. Ronan (who came here from Ireland in the 5th century) used to take every morning, barefoot and fasting.

_ PARDON OF ST. YVES,
TRÉGUIER _____

The St. Yves pardon is the pardon for the poor and for lawyers.

"Monsieur St. Yves" is Brittany's most popular saint, at once the redresser of wrongs and the consoler of the needy. Born at the manor house of Kermatin in 1253, Yves Helori studied law in Paris for thirteen years. On his return to Tréguier he was ordained into the priesthood, and practiced his profession as a magistrate and a lawyer— usually taking the defense in destitute cases. After his canonization in 1347 his fame spread far across the sea, and delegations of foreign lawyers still come every year to join the pilgrims in the pardon of the poor.

_ EMBROIDERY FESTIVAL,
PONT-L'ABBÉ _____

You have only to look at the splendid costumes to see how skillful these needle women are. It must be a true, inborn sense of beauty which thus bursts into golden flowers on the black velvet dresses of the women from Quimper, or runs riot in the complex curves of the Celtic decorative patterns.

And the sacred...

The Breton genius achieves its finest flowering in religious art. There are few other places where all artistic endeavor has been so tightly focused on a single ideal.

Romanesque Brittany was a wretched place and has bequeathed few notable buildings. But in the Gothic and Renaissance periods, under the sovereign dukes and later after the reunion with France, the countryside came to be covered in churches and chapels.

From the 15th to the 18th century a legion of Breton sculptors, working in stone or more commonly in wood, dedicated their finest work to the Church: pulpits, organ cases, baptisteries, choir stalls, rood beams and rood screens, altarpieces, statues, and the like. It was at this time also that the "parish close," which is the commonest form of monumental art in Breton communities, grew up around the church. Entered through a gate of honor, sometimes in the form of a Roman triumphal arch, the close comprises the church and its *placître*, the Calvary, and the ossuary. Here more than anywhere you will have occasion to wonder at the skill of the stonecutters, for the hard, tough granite is no easy material to work.

P. 54 L.

Church of Notre-Dame de la Joie, near Saint-Guénolé.

P. 63

Church at Plouha.

P. 94

Church of Trégarvan, Finistère.

P. 96 L. PARISH CLOSE, SAINT-THÉGONNEC

The acute rivalry between neighboring villages explains the splendor of the closes which were built in Lower Brittany in the Renaissance period and in the 17th century. Guimiliau and Saint-Thégonnec were deadly rivals for two centuries—during which they produced the two finest closes in the province.

The iconography of Saint-Thégonnec is, as usual, that of the Passion—but a little niche on the Calvary houses the patron saint, with the wolf which he harnessed to his cart after his donkey had been eaten by wolves.

In the crypt is a Holy Sepulcher carved in oak, dating from the late 17th century. In the church, the pulpit is a masterpiece of Breton sculpture. The 18th-century organs, while restored, still have their original pipes.

P. 97 CHURCH OF PLEYBEN: PARISH CLOSE

The Calvary is the most impressive in Brittany. Built in 1555 next to the church's side door, it was moved in 1738 and assumed its present position in 1743. There is a truly remarkable series of figures illustrating various episodes from the life of Jesus. The Last Supper shown here dates from 1650.

P. 98 L.

Josselin.

PP. 98 R., 99 MONASTERY OF POINTE SAINT-MATHIEU

These ruins are all that survives of a Benedictine monastery founded in the 6th century, where relics of St. Matthew brought back from Egypt by Breton sailors were said to be preserved.

The monastery was torn down during the Revolution, leaving only the huge abbey church (13th–16th century), which now forms part of the lighthouse buildings on pointe Saint-Mathieu.

PP. 100, 101 CAST CHURCH: ST. HUBERT'S HUNT

Better known than the church itself is the group known as "St. Hubert's Hunt," representing the saint with his squire and his two basset hounds. He is kneeling beside a minuscule horse before the stag, which bears the Cross between its horns.

P. 102 L. SAINT-TUGDUAL CATHEDRAL AT TRÉGUIER: TOMB OF ST. YVES

This is an 1890 reconstruction of the original erected by the duc Jean V in the 15th century, which was destroyed by the Etampes battalion.

P. 102 R. QUIMPER CATHEDRAL

A beautiful Gothic building whose choir dates from the 13th century, its nave and transept from the 15th; the towers, in the Breton style of the spire at Pont-Croix, were added only in the 19th century.

During the 16th-century wars of the League the nave was a place of refuge for the people of the region. Mass was celebrated there in such a welter of bedrolls, chests, and clothing that the plague broke out and killed 1,500 of the faithful.

The statue of Gradlon, king of Ys, stands between the two towers. An unusual feature of the building is that the choir and nave are not on the same axis.

_ P. 103 _____
Chapel of Saint-Egarec, Finistère.

_ P. 105 CHURCH OF SAINT-DERRIEN, COMMANA _____
This little church at the foot of the Arrée hills has the finest group of Baroque altarpieces in Brittany. The most remarkable is that of the altar of St. Anne (1682).

_ P. 106 L. HOLY-WATER STOUP, CHURCH OF LA MARTYRE _____
The parish close at La Martyre, built between the 14th and the 17th centuries, is the oldest in Léon. The ossuary (1619) has some strange, sinister decorations, including this sardonic figure of death, evoking Saint-Saëns's famous *Danse macabre*.

_ P. 106 R. NOTRE-DAME DE LA JOIE, PENMARC'H _____
This, the only seafarers' chapel near Bigoud, comes honestly by its title "Our Lady of Joy in Peril of the Sea." Built on the living rock, it has withstood wind and tide for four centuries. A sturdy, unpretentious 16th-century chapel, bare and chill, its nave like an upturned ship's hull, Notre-Dame was supposedly built to fulfill a vow by three crusaders of Picardy who fell into the hands of the Saracen chief Selim; they touched the heart of his daughter Ismeria, who helped them escape. Setting sail for France, they vowed to build a chapel to Our Lady on the first land they sighted—which was Penmarc'h.

_ P. 107 CHAPEL OF SAINT-SAMSON _
The chapel stands beside the pointe de Landunez in Finistère.

_ P. 108 L. NOTRE-DAME DE TRONOËN, SAINT-JEAN-TROLIMON _
This land-at-the-end-of-the-world fascinated the Gauls, who built a town here, as well as the Romans, who raised a temple to Venus Anadyomene (Rising from the Sea); later it became the site of Tronoën. The Calvary here is the oldest in Brittany, and others were modeled after it at Lampaul Guimiliau, Pleyben, and Plougastel-Daoulas. The altar stone, almost 18 feet in length, is said to be the largest in Christendom. With its turreted bell tower, Tronoën is one of the few chapels vaulted entirely in stone, whence its nickname, "the cathedral of the dunes."

_ P. 108 R. BELL TOWER OF NOTRE-DAME DE KROAS BATZ, ROSCOFF _
The bell towers of churches in Brittany served both a religious and a civil purpose, and were thus doubly dear to the people. Monarchs knew this well, and often pulled them down by way of punishment.

The remarkable Renaissance tower at Kroas Batz, with its lanterns, is one of the finest in Finistère.

_ P. 109 PARISH CLOSE, LAMPAUL GUIMILIAU _____
The parish close—triumphal entrance, funerary chapel, and Calvary—is the most typical form of monumental art in Breton towns. The concept, owing much to the profoundly mystical idea of "glorious death," is designed around the graveyard, usually entered through a triumphal gateway. Within stand the church and its *placître*, the Calvary, and the ossuary.

The *tref*, or rood beam across the triumphal arch at the junction of nave and choir, is the ancestor of the rood screen; to prevent the beam from sagging, it was supported by posts, which eventually gave way to an ornamental screen. This usually depicts scenes from the Passion, and always carries the group of Christ flanked by the Virgin and St. John.

_ P. 110 _____
Lichen-covered granite gargoyle.

_ P. 111 _____
Greece in Brittany—the church of Notre-Dame de Locmaria, Belle-Île-en-Mer.

_ P. 112 SAINT-THEY CHAPEL AND VIEW OF THE BAIE DES TRÉPASSÉS
Its bells once served to warn sailors of a perilous coast. On the cliff overlooking the Baie des Trépassés (Bay of the Departed) on the western side of the pointe du Van, this unpretentious little chapel is one of the most attractive on Cape Sizun. Most of the fabric dates from the 15th and 16th centuries. Outside, almost at the shore, are two fountains, one of them named for St. They; here, on pardon days, rheumatics came to bathe.

82-83

86-87

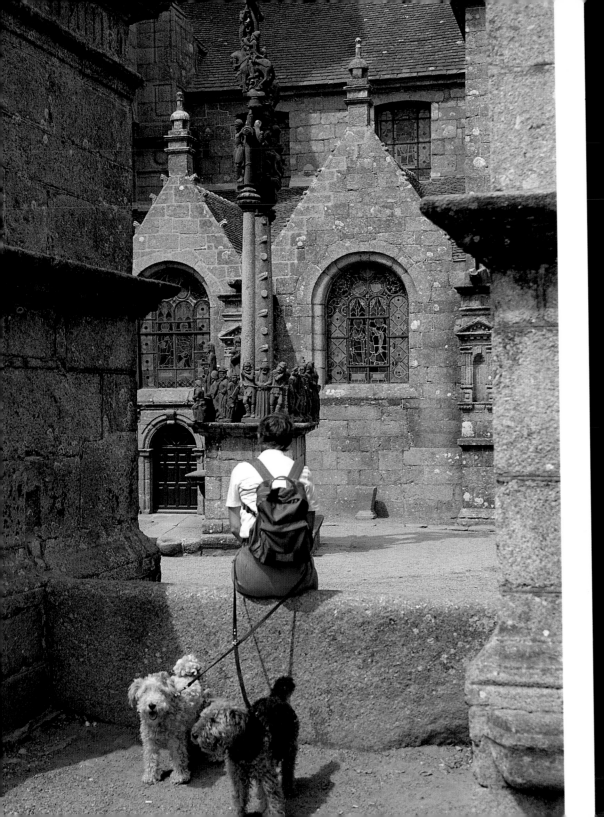
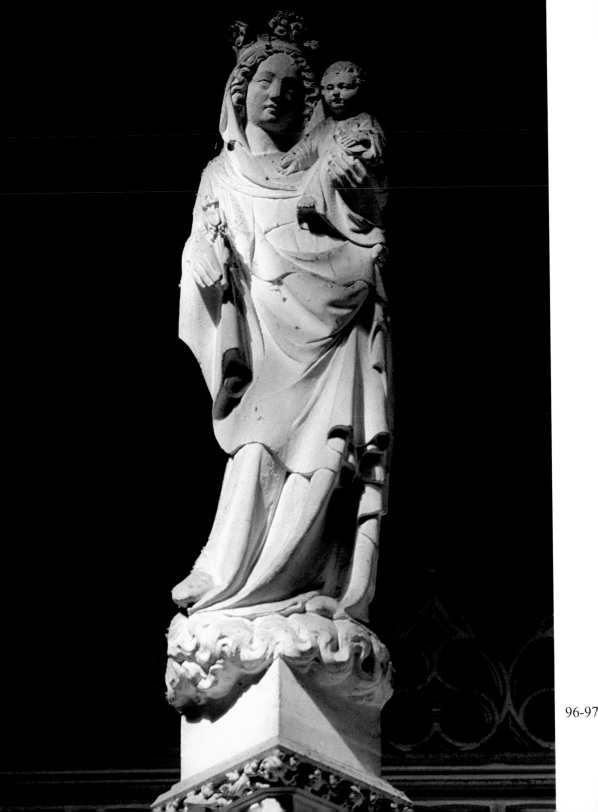

FAIST : A : BR : EST : PARMI V : OZA I : RCHETECTE

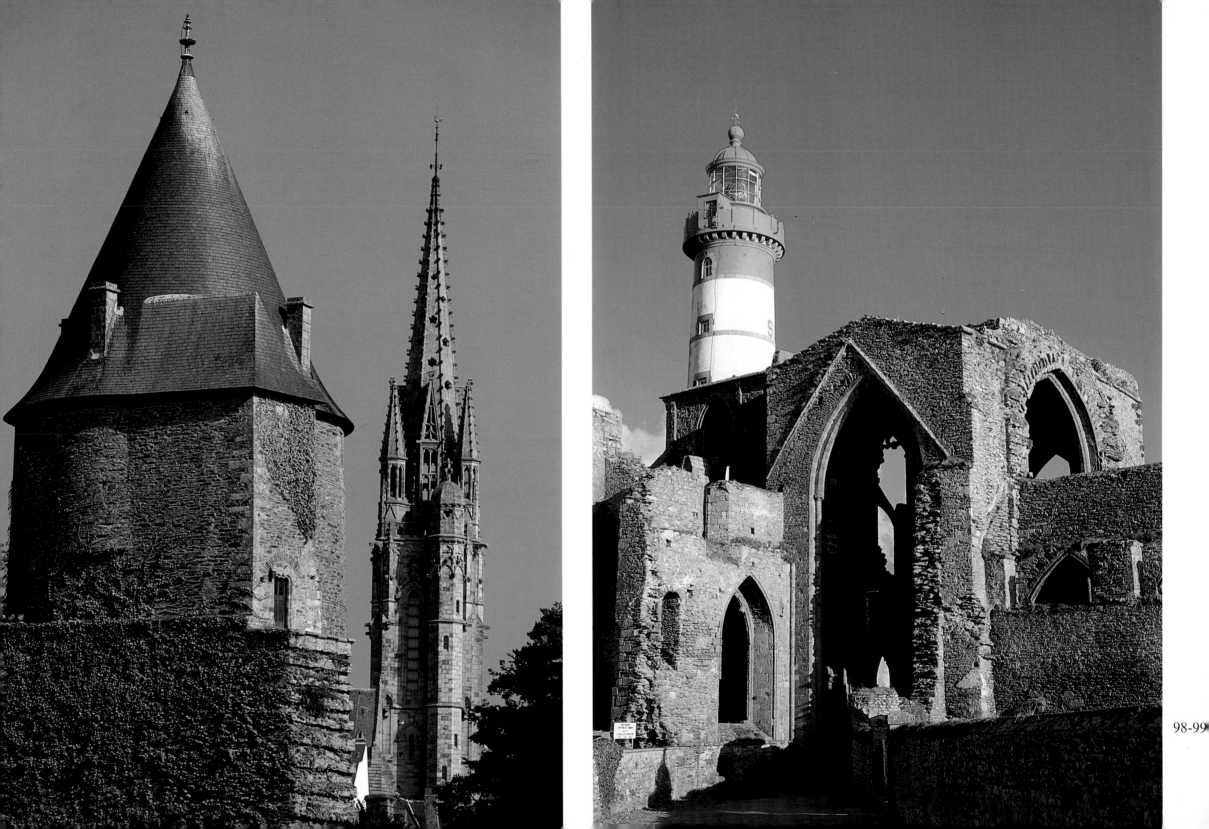

The Sea and the Granite

Lighthouses

Soon there will only be robots watching over the lives of men; the last keepers are leaving the lighthouses, and an entire era is going out with them.

More praise has been spoken of sailors than of these solitaries of the sea, these hermits who are nowadays winched down from a helicopter or up from a boat, but who once had to pick their way across the reefs to their tour of duty on an islet perhaps no bigger than a pocket handkerchief.

And what is to be said of the men who built such lighthouses in the open sea, like "La Vieille" (the Old Lady) or the "Ar-Men" light that marks the ill-omened Sein reef like a candle burning for the dead? It took fourteen years of frenzied toil to erect it on its sea-washed base.

Tomorrow's lighthouses may be more powerful and more scrupulously watchful. But in the dark night of the sea, sailors will no longer have the comfort of knowing that behind each of the warning lights along their course is a living man, waking and watching with them.

P. 121

Fort-La-Latte, on Cape Fréhel.

P. 122 CAPE FRÉHEL

Brittany's loveliest coastal upland, and one of the most beautiful places on the Emerald Coast. Now a bird sanctuary, it covers almost 750 acres of wild moorland, ending at a pink sandstone cliff which falls 230 feet to the sea, with the water boiling and foaming around the reefs at its base.

The view is magnificent, ranging from the pointe de Drouin on the right, with the Cotentin behind it, to the Île de Bréhat on the left. On a clear day you can even see the Channel Islands.

P. 123

Wild coastline, Quiberon.

P. 124

Trégastel.

PP. 126–136 BELLE-ÎLE

"Is there a height he may not climb?" was the motto of the *Grand Écureuil* (Great Squirrel), flagship of Nicolas Fouquet, Louis XIV's Superintendent of Finance (his name is an old word for squirrel). True to his motto, Fouquet set eyes on Belle-Île and made it his own, by purchase, in 1650. But the island's spell has bewitched many since; Courbet, Monet, Derain, Matisse, Flaubert, Sarah Bernhardt, Colette, and Arletty all came here for a change of scene. Not all its visitors came for pleasure; they included convicted criminals, and Acadians expelled from Canada by the British.

Belle-Île is the largest of the Ponant (Western) Islands, and indeed the largest island in Brittany, but its attraction does not lie in its size. It is said that no one can withstand its magic, that it is the island of everyone's dreams.

Some farming is done there; the Acadians brought the potato with them long before Parmentier popularized it on the mainland. There is also fishing, with one last sardine smack working the coastal waters. But the most important industry, bringing in almost 70 per cent of the island's revenues, is tourism. The Société Morbihannaise runs three ferries between Quiberon and Belle-Île; they make the 40-minute trip twelve times a day in each direction, carrying some 520,000 visitors a year.

P. 125
THE NEEDLES OF PORT-COTON

You'll be reminded of the pyramids of Cheops, Chefren, and Mycerinus, or of their smaller kinfolk—or you may think of the spine of some errant Loch Ness monster. These are the needles at Port-Coton, lace-edged towers of stone made familiar to museum goers by Claude Monet. The "cotton" in Port-Coton is said to allude to the white foam which the sea, for several thousand years past, has cast up around their feet.

PP. 127, 162 POINT AND LIGHTHOUSE, PONTUSVAL

In this tumbled landscape great blocks of granite stand house-high as though in an open field. These heaps of rock separate, and shelter, a series of small, sandy beaches at the foot of the bay of Pontusval.

_ *P. 128 LA VIEILLE (OLD WOMAN) LIGHTHOUSE, POINTE DU RAZ* _

This is truly the ends of the earth. As between the mainland, tailing off into slabs of stone and fragments of rock, and the ocean crashing against them, it is hard to tell which is gaining ground on the other.

_ *PP. 129, 158, 164 THE CÔTE DE GRANIT ROSE* _

Running the short distance from Perros-Guirec to Trébeurden, the Pink Granite Coast is one of Brittany's major tourist attractions. The views are spectacular; sandy beaches alternate with piles of copper-colored rocks lying along the ragged shoreline.

_ *P. 130 Port of Lorient* _

_ *P. 131* _

Port of Concarneau.

_ *P. 132* _

Port of Léchiagat.

_ *P. 133 LILIA FLATS, ÎLE-VIERGE LIGHTHOUSE* _

Built between 1897 and 1902, this is the highest lighthouse in France, rising 250 feet from its base and throwing its light an average of 33 miles. From the top, on a clear day, can be seen almost the whole coastline of Finistère—from Ushant to the Île de Batz.

_ *P. 134* _

Audierne.

_ *P. 135* _

Low neap tide at Aber Wrac'h.

_ *P. 137* _

Is it in memory of Fouquet's flagship, *Le Grand Écureuil* (The Great Squirrel), that the *Belem* today flies the colors of the Squirrel?

_ *PP. 138, 139, 141 ECKMÜHL LIGHT-HOUSE, POINTE DE PENMARC'H* _

This lighthouse stands at the tip of Penmarc'h Point. Built in 1897, it stands 210 feet high; its two-million-candlepower-beacon throws light an average of 34 miles.

The construction funds were a gift from the marquise de Blocqueville, daughter of Marshal Davout, the prince of Eckmühl. There is a splendid view over the bay of Audierne, the pointe du Raz, the coast at Concarneau, and the Glénan archipelago.

_ *P. 140 THE GREAT LIGHTHOUSE OF BELLE-ÎLE* _

Belle-Île ("beautiful island") is the subject of an old saw: "See Belle-Île and you've seen the island you long for." Many have done so: Sarah Bernhardt, Monet, Courbet, Derain, Matisse, Flaubert, Colette, and Arletty all came here for a change of scene, captivated by the great lighthouse standing between Goulphar and the shelter of Port-Donnant.

The light began operations in 1835. It is 150 feet high, but the chamber is a full 295 feet above sea level, and the throw of 75 miles is one of the longest in Europe.

The toilers of the sea

"Does the billow spare the man when, on a wild night of winter, it sweeps through the reef bearing kelp to enrich his barren fields? No; it is often the same wave that sweeps the wrack ashore and the man out to sea."

So says Jules Michelet, but literature abounds in praise of sailors and seamen.

It is partly the kind of romantic image which flowers readily along Brittany's wild coast; but there is truth in it too, since the seafarer's callings are indeed perilous. As we have seen in recent years, our huge floating factories are as much at the mercy of the elements as the little skiffs of time past. Death is a familiar of these shores, not merely a figure of speech or the morose invention of poets crossed in love. He belongs here as much as wind and water.

Only those born to the sea can be content to live by it. It takes as much love as need to make a sailor.

THE GOÉMON HARVEST

A horse walks through water above his hocks, laboriously dragging a cart from which hang tangles of dripping seaweed.... The right to gather *goémon* (kelp) is reserved exclusively for seamen by trade; it is a sea crop, and it belongs to those who make their living from the sea.

Nowadays the harvest is mostly gathered with cranes and tractors, but here and there small farmers still gather kelp in the traditional way, hauling it in carts to spread on the barren fields.

SHELLFISH GATHERING

Huge beds of scallops were found in 1960 in the bay of Saint-Brieuc, and shell-fishing has made a comeback. Trawlers from Erquy and Saint-Cast drag for clams and scallops all along the coast. Over the beds, the trawl is thrown out so that it sweeps the sea floor and is then brought back aboard. The net is emptied onto the deck, and the crew separate the shellfish from the pebbles brought up with them. Bivalves which have not yet reached legal size are thrown back.

Spider crabs are also taken all along the coast and immediately put in salt-water pens to await sale.

Lobsters are found on the rocky bottom farther offshore; Bretons traditionally catch them in lobster pots baited with fresh fish. But since the harvest is declining, fishermen are venturing farther afield; the lobster boats of Camaret, Audierne, and Douarnenez spend months off the coast of Mauretania, where they freeze part of their catch on board. When they return to shore, the live lobsters are placed in salt-water pens which are found all along the coast, particularly between Primel and Audierne.

SHELLFISH FARMING

Oysters:
It takes four years, divided into three principal phases, to raise an oyster. First, the spat is transplanted to underwater growing posts. A year or two later comes the "swap," which involves removing the young oyster from its support (and its neighbors) with wooden shears. For the second phase the oysters are arranged on steel trays in growing areas, and here they attain their adult size. At the end of the year the grower can either sell them as deep-sea oysters or cull them, as is usually done, for fattening. The fattening areas are to be found on the Channel coast, near Cancale and Morlaix.
Mussels:
Natural-bed mussels grow in Mont-Saint-Michel bay, Saint-Brieuc bay, and the Vilaine estuary. Cultured mussels are raised in the Aven, on Île Tudy, and at Croisic.

OCEAN FISHING

Trawlers are the mainstay of fresh-fish supplies for mass consumption. Once they went after white tuna *(germon)* in the gulf of Gascony; now they have to go out to mid-Atlantic after red tuna, using nets which cover many acres to drag the catch back to the freezer ships.

This is the main business of such fishing ports as Lorient, Douarnenez, and Concarneau.

DEEP-SEA FISHING

Perhaps the best-known kind of fishing, in reality and legend both, is for cod on the banks of Newfoundland, Labrador, and Greenland. Long ago it made the fame and fortune of Paimpol and Saint-Malo (the last port from which it is still practiced today). The boats set out for Newfoundland in early January, with a crew of sixty, and stay for three months. When they return to port, they lie up for three weeks before going out again.

COASTAL FISHING

There are no longer flapping sails, but at high tide you can still see the fishing boats making for port, heavy with their loads of mullet, turbot, skate, or sardine. Coastal fishing is the commonest; it supplies the whole Breton coast with fresh fish. Between tides it's time for maintenance work on boats and equipment.

_PP. 142, 143 _____
Trawlers in Concarneau harbor.

_P. 144 _____
The harbor at Dahouët on the Flora estuary, Côtes d'Armor.

_P. 145 _____
Wreck at Audierne.

_PP. 146, 147
OYSTER BEDS AT CANCALE _____
Cancale enjoys a high reputation for its cultured oysters. Since 1920, when a mysterious blight decimated the banks from which the spat was drawn, only Auray oysters are raised here, but efforts are being made to reestablish the indigenous variety, which is grown offshore and has a very special flavor due to the high plankton content of Mont-Saint-Michel bay.

_P. 148 _____
Kelp gathering at Pointe de l'Arcouest.

_P. 149 ABER WRAC'H _____
Unlike the Spanish loanword ria, aber is of Celtic origin. There are abers along the northwest coast of Finistère, called the "coast of legend." Much shallower than the estuaries of the north coast, like those of the Morlaix, Jaudy, and Trieux rivers, the abers are the channels not of rivers but of small streams that could not of themselves cut a way through the silt. Thus there are no important harbors on the abers such as those found at the head of an estuary (Morlaix or Dinan). All this low-lying, rocky coast is rich in kelp, most of it processed in local plants. Aber Wrac'h is an important pleasure harbor for sailboats; it also has a merchant marine school.

_P. 150 LES SEPT ÎLES:
ÎLE AUX OISEAUX _____
Bird Island's real name is Rouzic, and along with Malban and Bono, it belongs to the Seven Islands archipelago. It became a bird sanctuary in 1911 and the public is not allowed to land here, but birdwatching launches sail around the island. From these you can see the impressive gannet population (about 4,000 pairs) at Bassan, which summers there from June through September. From May to July there are guillemots, Torda penguins, brown-backed, silver, and deep-sea gulls, crested cormorants, puffins, kittiwakes, oyster-catchers, and a few fulmars.

_P. 151 _____
Lobster ponds at Mogueriec, near Roscoff.

_P. 152
CONCARNEAU: A CITY ENCLOSED _
This is a crescent-shaped island in its own sheltering cove, linked to the mainland by two little bridges with a fortification between them. The curtain walls, flanked by two towers, were raised by the dukes of Brittany between 1451 and 1476 outside an earlier 14th-century wall.

The work, more than 1,200 feet long and 325 feet deep, is surrounded by a rampart with nine towers, the principal defenses lying outside the west gate. This is the most vulnerable point, being nearest to the mainland and uncovered at low tide.

Pastimes and harbors

Whether excelling as merchants, pirates, royal privateers, Napoleon's bluejackets, deep-sea fishermen, or single-handed sailors around the world, Bretons have always ruled the waves.

In times past they were called Jacques Cartier, Porcon de la Bardinais, Duguay Trouin, and Surcouf. Today they bear such names as Tabarly, Poupon, Morvan, or Kersauzon. From rum-running to the America's Cup, by way of the Figaro Race and the Sailors' Tour de France, they continue to add to their laurels; Deroff and Henard were France's only gold medalists at the last Olympics. But Brittany, though the nursery of champions, is not for champions only; it has much to offer to novices and seasoned amateurs as well. Along these 750 miles of jagged coastline there are opportunities for almost every conceivable kind of water sport. To the north is the Emerald Coast, sprinkled with rocks and islets, and the bay of Saint-Malo where the rise and fall of the tide is enough to take a boat up the Rance estuary as far as Dinan, where it can enter the Breton canal system. The Pink Granite Coast is a succession of white-sand beaches and coppery boulders, backed by 220 miles of navigable estuaries and rivers. Then comes Finistère with its rugged capes, for those who love sensational effects; the islands for maritime puttering and trolling; then Morbihan with its enormous beaches and its wild, rocky, wave-beaten shores. In Brittany you can try, or learn, any water sport: dinghy sailing, canoeing, sailboarding, sea kayaking, speedboat racing, funboarding, sand-yachting, sport-catamaran sailing, diving, spearfishing—it's all there; you have only to choose, and to dare.

_ P. 153 _____

Church of Notre-Dame de la Joie in the
village of Saint-Guénolé, pointe de
Penmarc'h.

_ PP. 154, 155, 171
POINTE DE LA TORCHE _____

Contrary to expectation the name, which
translates roughly as Lantern Head, has
nothing to do with a source of light, whether
a lighthouse or some other. It is simply a
corrupt pronunciation of the Breton Beg an
Dorchenn, or Flat Stone Point. It is crowned
by a tumulus with an important dolmen, a
landmark for sailboard enthusiasts who head
for it through the breakers.

_ P. 156 _____

Morgat harbor.

_ P. 157 _____

Sailboat festival at Concarneau.

_ PP. 159, 163 _____

Horseback riding on the Plage des Rosaires.

_ P. 160 _____

Beach at Pors-ar-Vag, Plomediern.

_ P. 161 BAIE DES TRÉPASSÉS _____

Girt by the twin heads of Cape Sizun, the
pointe du Raz and the pointe due Van, is
the Bay of the Departed. A byword for
shipwreck and death, it is said to be haunted
by the drowned on their way to the next
world. Whether they are Dahut's brave
sailors "whose kiss would slay a lover," or
poor Christians caught in the snares of
Morgan le Fay, it is here that they must
wander until the end of time.

Oddly enough, this legend of death should
really be coupled with the land rather than
the sea. In Breton "Boe an Anaon," the bay
of souls in torment, the Baie des Trépassés is
supposed to have once been the port of
embarkation for dead Druids on their way to
burial on the Île de Sein.

_ P. 165 _____

Sunset at Trébeurden.

_ P. 166 ÎLE DE BRÉHAT _____

Twenty-two miles long by 9½ wide, Bréhat
comprises two islands joined in the 18th
century, thanks to the great military engineer
Vauban, by the Ar Prat bridge. The
shoreline here is very craggy, surrounded by
reefs and islets. Its gentle climate makes it a
lovely place, and all the more so because
motor vehicles are not allowed.

_ PP. 167, 178
THE PINK GRANITE COAST _____

The beach of Saint-Guirec at Ploumanac'h
and the château de Costaeres. Ploumanac'h,
famous for its tumbled rocks, is now a
popular resort. The beach lies on the bay of
Saint-Guirec, named for the Celtic evangelist
who landed here from Britain in the 6th
century. There is a granite statue of him,
replacing the original wood carving which,
over the centuries, had been robbed of an
important part of its anatomy by generations
of young women: if you wanted a husband,
you twisted the saint's nose!

The château, built in the 19th century,
stands on the Île de Costaeres across from
Saint-Guirec beach. Henryk Sienkiewicz,
who won the Nobel Prize for literature in
1905 and wrote historical novels of which the
best-known is Quo Vadis?, once stayed here.

_ P. 168 _____

Sand-yachts on the beach at Plounéour-Trez.

_ P. 169 _____

Sailing instruction on Rosary Beach.

_ P. 170 LÉZARDRIEUX HARBOR _____

This little town lies on the left bank of the
Jaudy which, with the Trieux, delimits the
"wild peninsula" on which it stands. A
suspension bridge carries the road to
Paimpol across an arm of the sea.

_ PP. 172, 173 _____

The Figaro Race at Perros-Guirec.

_ P. 176 ERQUY _____

Lying at the foot of an open bay giving on to
the gulf of Saint-Brieuc and sheltered by
high sandstone cliffs, Erquy has become one
of the most important scallop-fishing centers
in Côtes d'Armor.

The fast-growing town also boasts some
very fine beaches, notably that at Caroual,
from which the view over bay and headland
is unsurpassed.

_ P. 177 _____

Ploumanac'h.

_ P. 179 _____

Castle Point, Plougrescant.

_ P. 180 PORT-LOUIS:
TOWN AND CITADEL _____

This strong point commands the entrance to
Lorient roadstead. It was begun in 1591,
during the Spanish occupation, by Don Juan
del Aguila, continued by Marshal de Brissac,
and completed in 1636 by order of Richelieu.

Since it owed its advancement to Louis XIII, the then town of Blavet assumed the name Port-Louis as a mark of gratitude. Its prosperity was due to the establishment here of the Compagnie des Indes (the French East India Company), before it moved to Lorient.

In the keep is the Company's naval museum, with displays covering maritime history in the Atlantic.

_ PP. 182, 183 SAINT-SERVAN: HARBOR AND SOLIDOR TOWER

Solidor used to be the naval port for Saint-Servan sur Mer. In the 14th century a fortress was built here by the duc Jean IV to guard the Rance and blockade Saint-Malo. The Solidor Tower commands the entrance to the Rance estuary. After serving as a prison, it is now the Musée International du Long Cours et des Cap Horniers, with displays illustrating round-the-world, and particularly round-the-Horn, navigation under sail.

And some others:

_ SAINT-QUAY-PORTRIEUX

A coastal resort known since the Dark Ages, since St. Quay landed here from Wales around 470. The port, once a base for the Newfoundland fleet, now has only one flotilla of fishing boats, but it has been expanded with an enormous deep-water marina.

Saint-Quay-Portrieux is also the site of an international saltwater fishing championship held here every year.

_ BINIC

Binic is a charming sea resort, where cod fishing boats once wintered. Now its harbor is used only by pleasure boats and a few coastal fishing vessels.

_ POINTE DE SAINT-CAST

Here at land's end, where sky and sea meet, there is a monument to the memory of "those who fled from France, choosing rather to die on their feet than to live on their knees." It is a challenge to the traveler, and we may well believe that many, like Baudelaire, have dreamed of the joys of going "down there" to live together under a burning sky and a steaming sun.

_ PENTHIÈVRE PENINSULA AND FORT (QUIBERON PENINSULA)

In the summer of 1795 thousands of Royalist émigrés, protected by a British naval squadron, made one last attempt at a landing on French soil here in the Quiberon peninsula. Reinforced by Cadoudal's Chouans, they put up a stiff resistance to Republican forces before being overwhelmed by General Hoche on his way to "pacify" the Vendée.

The fort at Penthièvre, restored in the 19th century, commands the neck of the peninsula and was thus the scene of many engagements. A monument and a crypt recall fifty-nine members of the Resistance who were shot here in 1944.

_ BEACH OF L'ÉCLUSE (THE LOCK), DINARD

Marcel Proust turned Cabourg into his Balbec; he could just as well have picked Dinard, with its magnificent site at the mouth of the Rance opposite Saint-Malo.

Launched in the mid-19th century by an American named Coppinger, Dinard has become a fashionable sea resort with an international clientele. The Ecluse beach lies between the Moulinet and Malouine points.

_ BAY OF MORLAIX

Not all Breton cities live exclusively on fishing. Since the mid-18th century Morlaix has had a tobacco factory. Originally founded by the French East India Company, it still turns out every year 300 million cigars, 50 tons of chewing tobacco, and 15 tons of snuff. Obviously tobacco chewing and snuff taking are not nearly as obsolete as has been supposed.

128-1

132-1

136-1

138-1

.22
.20
.18
.16

146-1

148-1

152-1

154-1

156-1

162-1

174-17

178-1

180-1

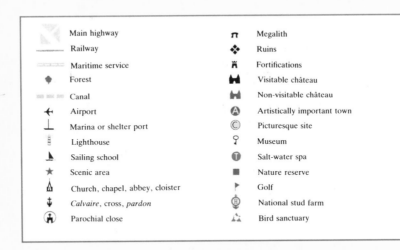 Main highway		π	Megalith
Railway		❖	Ruins
Maritime service			Fortifications
Forest			Visitable château
Canal			Non-visitable château
Airport		Ⓐ	Artistically important town
Marina or shelter port		Ⓒ	Picturesque site
Lighthouse			Museum
Sailing school		Ⓣ	Salt-water spa
★ Scenic area		■	Nature reserve
Church, chapel, abbey, cloister			Golf
Calvaire, cross, *pardon*			National stud farm
Parochial close			Bird sanctuary

Ile d'Ouessant

Lampaul ○   ★

Ile Molène

POINTE D

C O T E   S U D   -   F I

Ile de

Br